WHO'S
BEHIND THE
Curtain
FOR YOU?

HOW TO USE YOUR STORIES
AND START SELLING YOU

NANCY HOPPER

Who's Behind the Curtain for You?
How to Use Your Stories and Start Selling You

ISBN 10: 0692152148

ISBN 13: 9780692152140

Cover Painting – Jill Pankey

Book and Cover Design – Lisa Thomson

Acknowledgements

Who's Behind the Curtain for YOU began from an experience I had when I was five years old. Yes, way back then. That event gave me a belief in myself which has lasted throughout my life. So it is with a lifetime of gratitude that I thank the Filipino nun, Sister Margarita who coached me (from behind the curtain) and made me a STAR. That propelled me to success in building long-term relationships, engaging with others in finding a common thread to fall in love with people, using my life's funny stories to relate to men and women all over, seeing humor in so many of my sales experiences and turning those into win-win situations.

My Dad was an entertainer and storyteller with an engaging personality and loved all people. I believe he is the one who taught me to "fall in love with people." I would not be who I am today without his strong influence in my life, a real-life character filled with love, respect of others, and stories!

My Mother who we all call our little BEBO is a spit-fire of fun and is my best friend. Her loving care is what made the "My Mother" poem, by Ann Taylor, a reality.

This book would not have been possible without the UNSTOPPABLE direction, kindness, encouragement, and love of my husband, Mel. We are known as the yin and the yang of the family. Mel has a "servant's heart," and he is my "Paul Bunyan." As I was writing this book, Mel kept telling me over and over again when I wrote, "keep going, you have a lot of wood to chop!"

I am blessed to have a giving, caring, and yes, patient family who are there for me through thick and thin. My children Laura Ann and Aaron Ace have strong personalities with huge hearts. I am so proud of how they have become accomplished and compassionate adults. They were the ones responsible for my success-driven Mompreneur era!

Ms. Barbara Tidwell, the founder of the Texas State University Strutters Dance Team, who mentored me during my college era. She taught how to look someone in the eye and have a firm TEXAS handshake, and that a smile wins every time.

Grace Fletcher, my niece took my pictures and Bonnie Downs, her sister was supportive from the get go. These two nieces are tied to my hip because they have been a great inspiration in the long journey of what is possible.

Jill Pankey is my dearest friend from college. She is creative, talented, and generous. Jill is the artist who created the painting for the cover of the book. Jill shared her personal story of 'who had been behind the curtain for her.' Jill has a strength and a desire to help capture people's lives. www.jillpankey.com

A thanks goes out to Tom Julian, JUL-TV, the muscle behind my book. He is a visionary with heart and mentors so many in helping them also have success in their lifetime.

NSA-Austin Chapter had a writing class that I attended in November 2017. This was my first time to write since my college days, and they taught me so much in three days!

In addition to those mentioned above, there are a number of individuals who also supported and helped to make this book shine – Khrisana Edwards, Pamela Hosch, Kathy Langdon, Olivia Benloulou, Lisa Thomson, and last but NOT least, KAREN MCCULLOUGH.

Karen has been a tremendous MENTOR for me. Owning her accomplishments is a story in itself. She is the first one to give me a job to re-enter in the sales industry. Karen is a national keynote speaker, entertainer and helps so many in their journey to success. Her natural talent, humor and the clarity she directed in guiding me through this journey are second to none. Karen, thank you for making my dream come to life on and off the pages.

NANCY HOPPER
KEYNOTE SPEAKER/AUTHOR
[cid: 974A7A72-4C05-444B-B3DD-7F2FFC68F00]
512.745.5081
nancy@nancyhopper.com

Contents

Introduction

As the famous songwriter and cultural icon Bob Dylan said in the early 60's, "THE TIMES, THEY ARE A'CHANGING." Well, I am sure he had no clue when he said and sang that line just how much the times would change over the next 50 years. Because of technology, an even greater change has taken place going into the 21st century.

The internet and social media has opened up a myriad of competition for those who are in outside sales. Nowadays, everyone could be working offsite instead of at their home office. The person who makes the decision to purchase or buy maybe sitting in front of their computer three time zones away; however, what has NOT changed is that the customer's decision to buy comes down to a strong internal 'gut' feeling. This final determining factor in the sales decision process is an EMOTION, not a DATA FACT.

In my book I will share stories from my sales career to give you the necessary sales strategies and techniques to successfully interface with your clients or customers. At the end of each chapter I will summarize the lessons and

To me there is just "ONE SECRET" I learned that can make your career in sales a success.

techniques expressed with humor and techniques that work! To me there is just "ONE SECRET" I learned that can make your career in sales a success. The power of learning to connect with your clients and prospective customers, of how to be a closer and keeping those WOW

CLIENTS, has only been available from my sales and motivational and keynote speeches.

I have been honored that my audiences throughout the years have RELATED, REMEMBERED AND RETOLD my stories. And they are true and funny! Now I am sharing some of my favorite stories where I have experienced mentoring, building relationships and selling to others. This will give you a written path to success. I hope this path will make your success a little easier by helping you to learn what works without having to experience what doesn't work.

Of course we can all be better storytellers! I hope you will use my stories, add your stories to your own career in closing more deals!

Let's get started together!

Hopper

Chapter One

Who's Behind the Curtain for YOU

No matter what profession you choose in life, one has to start somewhere and climb up the "learning curve" to obtain the knowledge and experience in being successful. Remember, everyone needs a MENTOR or some type of support to keep them pointed in the right direction and moving forward to success.

I was very lucky—I was the only girl in my family and my father thought I could do anything. My Dad was an ARMY MAN and my family moved to where ever Uncle Sam needed him. Having started my career at the early age of five on a parochial school stage in Taiwan was luck.

The nuns put on a Mother's Day program, and as you may know, NUNS LOVE PRODUCTIONS! We were to honor our Mothers and I had the lead part; basically, I was the star. My special nun was SISTER MARGARITA and I was NOT to tell my parents or a soul about the upcoming production, not to practice at home especially. This might have been the

> *Remember, everyone needs a MENTOR or some type of support to keep them pointed in the right direction and moving forward to success.*

3

only SECRET I have ever kept in my childhood, because I was so scared of the nuns.

Mother's Day came and my parents were sitting in the midst of the other parents and had no idea what was going to happen. The program started and I walked out to the microphone in the middle of the stage. I looked at the giant silver stick and began reciting the poem, "My Mother" by Ann Taylor.

"Who fed me from her gentle breast
and hush'd me in her arms to rest.
And on my sweet cheek sweet kisses pressed?
MY MOTHER"

This poem was twenty-four verses long and I did not pause or skip a beat. I blew the audience away, especially my parents. As they were listening to me, they looked at each other in total amazement. Then asked each other, "When did Nancy memorize this poem?" "Did you see her do it at the house?" They were both shocked and could not believe I did it. Knowing my personality, not really a student of reading, believe me, it was a shock to see such a performance.

This poem was twenty-four verses long and I did not pause or skip a beat.

From that day I loved the stage. I had all of the confidence in the world. I loved getting up in front of groups of people or strangers; well, you get the picture. Talking to people was like "water on a duck's back." Easy. As the years went on, when a school teacher, Sunday School teacher or a sales manager asked for someone to give a speech, or network for new prospects, my hand went up first. I learned and developed what I called my "people skills."

As a little girl, I loved to exaggerate and embellish things that happened to me. So when I looked back on my starring role in the Catholic Mother's Day Program, my performance was short of an Oscar.

Many years later I began my speaking career with the National Association of Speakers in NSA Houston, Texas. I saw an ad in a magazine where a little five year old girl who had pigtails was holding a phone to her ear. The ad was for Southwestern Bell saying, "Call me, I got started EARLY talking on the phone!"

There was Sister Margarita, from BEHIND THE CURTAIN, and the only thing showing was her white habit and her black shoes.

When I saw this advertisement, I remembered my Mother had a black and white photo of me at the age of five speaking on that stage into that big silver microphone. This was my famous Mother's Day Production! I too had gotten started EARLY! I quickly called my mom and asked her to 'dig' it up so I could use it in my promotional material for speaking opportunities.

It was going to be fantastic and say, "Some of us got started early! START NOW! Let Nancy Hopper set the stage for your business. Nancy has been inspiring and motivating audiences for the past twenty years. She will EXPLODE your next sales meeting and convention! Don't use dynamite, call DYNOHOP!" Once I got the postcard back I was with my Mother, so excited to share with her what I had done with the old postcard picture. Then we both looked at the front of that postcard picture and busted out laughing! There was Sister Margarita, from BEHIND THE CURTAIN, and the only thing showing was her white habit and her black shoes. She was there to support me, calling out the words to the poem, every sentence, wanting no recognition or praise. She wanted to make sure I was successful. I then remembered when I did hesitate or stopped she would throw me a word or sentence to make me look like a STAR.

Sure enough, that bat was released from her little hands and flew backwards to hit me square in the MOUTH.

And this next story is when my sales career really took off. I was ten years old, my Dad was assigned to Fort Sam Houston in San Antonio, Texas, and that is where I grew up. Having two brothers, I was a real "tomboy" and loved sports.

During the spring sometimes my girlfriends and I would meet at someone's home and play baseball in their front yard, hoping just maybe some boys would ride their bikes by and see our athletic abilities.

We would rotate positions, and there were only three of us, so it went pretty darn fast in the rotation. I was up for catcher and standing further back than normal. Batter UP, and she took a swing. Sure enough, that bat was released from her little hands and flew backwards to hit me square in the MOUTH. As most of you know and have experienced a facial and mouth wound, it bleeds profusely. The girls went screaming into the home and here came the Mom. She took one look at me and screamed, ran in, got a towel with ice and a phone to call my parents.

I called my home and my Dad picked up, most likely watching sports on TV. I told him what happened and to come pick me up. We were only 2-3 minutes away, and it seemed I waited a long time. He finally drove up. I was sitting on their porch and he got out of his car, slowly.

We are going to go door to door and sell those hot pads for fifty cents each!"

I began to walk towards him and he stopped once he saw my face and mouth. And in a strong concerned voice he said, "A BASEBALL DID THAT??" Then through my crying and swollen mouth, missing teeth I said, "NO, a BASEBALL BAT!"

As my parents hurried to get me in to see a dentist on this Sunday afternoon, I was told I could not go to school for a while. Having to wait for the swelling to go down and then begin some major repair work from several dentists was in my future. I pretty well hid out because I did not want anyone to see me, of course. And if my parents ever thought before this accident that I might never get married, I knew now, they laid in bed and whispered to each other, "for sure, she will never get married."

So off to the back room, my bedroom, I went for weeks. Watching TV and listening to my radio could entertain me just for so long. I was driving my mom crazy as she was a substitute school teacher and a stay at home mother. Leaving me by myself and wanting to keep me busy, she had a good idea for me. It was a handcrafter one. Mom bought a loom to hand weave and make these little hot pads! There were made from multi-colored pastel colors, pink, blue—just beautiful. It did take my mind off of my face and mouth and gave me something to do instead of eat ice cream and watch "I Love Lucy." I must have made at least 100 of these hot pads, more than any of my mother's friends could ever use in a lifetime.

"Once I teach you how to sell, you will always be able to take care of yourself."

Then it happened. One Friday afternoon, my dad walked by my room and noticed all of my talent. And then he stopped at my door and said, "Nancy, I'm going to teach you how to sell tomorrow, Saturday. We are going to go door to door and sell those hot pads for fifty cents each!" I was totally taken back as I was only ten. This is the last thing I thought I would be doing in my healing process. Heck, I had sold some Girl Scout cookies, and I ate most of those. Now here I was going to go door to door selling these pastel hot pads and my mouth was still so messed up.

In fact, when I spoke it was more like I had a harelip, with a slight droop to a corner of my mouth. No joke.

Then my Dad said a line that has stayed with me my whole life in sales. "ONCE I TEACH YOU HOW TO SELL, YOU WILL ALWAYS BE ABLE TO TAKE CARE OF YOURSELF." That's when I looked up at him from my warm bed, with hot pads all around me and said, "Daddy, I want to be like Mommy. She does not sell and seems to be very happy."

Well my Dad was a career military guy and his kids obeyed orders and we did what he said to do. He had served in World War II, Korea and Vietnam. But he loved sports and coached high school aged kids in tennis from the time I could remember. He was a great guy. Oh, and he loved to sell, talk to people, entertain them and the game of tennis was his game of life.

On that next morning, Saturday came...and he said, "gather up your hot pads and put them in this bag your mom gave you. Let's go and WE'LL HAVE SOME FUN!"

We got in the family car and literally drove down my street to the end. I don't know what happened to the WE part of this selling; however, I do know he was sitting in the car, smoking a cigarette and told me, "this is what you are going to say and do." HE SCRIPTED ME! Then before I could reach for the handle of this Wildcat Buick, to bust out of the car, my Dad said, "WAIT, we have to PRACTICE!"

My Dad was right! SELLING WAS FUN!

I then slowly got out of this big-ass car, his window down, smiling at me, taking his hand and waving me on, with a big smile.

I was a sight to be seen. A little chubby fat girl, with a bad home perm, could not pronounce my words enough to be audible. My hot pads were in this brown paper sack (cute, Mom)...and then I approached the first door. I rang the doorbell. Great, I thought, no one home. Then I heard someone walking to the door and there I was, swollen lips, teeth crushed and my script was ready to go.

And the script went like this: With a big smile, "Hi, I am Nancy Fletcher and live on this street. I have been busy making these handmade hot pads since I can't go to school right now. They are seventy-five cents each or you can buy two for an extra quarter!" Then my Dad told me to wait for their response. Seriously, they took one look at my face and mouth and said as fast as they could, I will take two of those hot pads" and then gave me a DOLLAR! As quick as they could shut the door, I said, "THANK YOU!" BOOM!

Turning around to make sure my dad was still in the car, watching me, I smiled and went to the next house, and every house on that side of the street. He moved his car slowly up the street, following me. I sold all of the hot pads and had more spending money than I had ever had before. Babysitting at ten years old was also fifty cents except it was an HOUR to make your two quarters!

My dad was right! SELLING WAS FUN!

A number of years went by and I had caps on my front teeth and I joined everything I could in high school. I worked to be friends with everybody. When someone showed up new to our school from junior high to high school, I couldn't wait to show them around and make them feel comfortable in their new school. However, I had never been a leader in any of my school class wide activities. Well, once I was voted in to be a school reporter but didn't report anything. That didn't last long.

One day in my junior year I decided to go out for one of the senior cheerleader positions. I came home the night before tryouts and announced to my family my important decision. My dad, who was always confident in my abilities (let's not forget the POEM story), was somewhat taken back. He said, "I know you have lots of energy and can YELL, but can you do anything else?" I stood in this small living room and did a cheer and a big hurdle, flipped right there in this tiny space, and said, "What do you think now?"

I really wanted to be a cheerleader and I gave it all my passion and energy that next week before the voting. I put everything on the line, used all my selling skills. The announcement time came and I made that senior spot, which was my first big goal for myself.

Looking back, the positive influence of my dad, he was the "BEHIND THE CURTAIN FOR ME" from the beginning. And not leaving out my mother, for sure, she

Some of us just got started early... START NOW! LET NANCY HOPPER SET THE STAGE FOR YOUR BUSINESS

was the silent support that has always been there for me and still is to this day.

1. You have to BELIEVE in yourself and have confidence.

2. Being SCRIPTED is for PROS.

3. When you show PASSION and ENERGY for what you are selling, people will be attracted to YOU...no matter what you look like!

Chapter Two

Nothing To Lose

As a young married couple, two years out of college with only one income and a two-year-old baby girl, we had the typical newlywed problems. We had too many bills and not enough income. We needed some additional steady income to make ends meet.

One Sunday while my daughter was down for her nap, I put on *60 Minutes*. They were doing a segment on the Tupperware phenomenon that was sweeping across the nation. It showed happy housewives and young mothers having parties to sell Tupperware. They showed the

> *I wanted to be the number one sales person for Tupperware in the state of Texas.*

company having weekly sales rallies, bonuses being given out and cars being earned. This was just what I needed: 1) Extra income 2) Time with other adult women 3) Time away from my family 4) A chance to earn a second car and a job that motivated you to succeed.

Monday morning could not come fast enough. I called the local Austin Tupperware distributorship and made an appointment for an interview as early as possible. I quickly signed up. I was all in and I was determined to be a success. I wanted to be the number one sales person for

Tupperware in the state of Texas. After that, I wanted to be number one in the nation—which meant I had to start learning what it would take to be number one.

In the beginning, I had to learn Tupperware's sales and business procedures and techniques. I had to be coachable and absorb everything they taught me. I learned to do everything by protocol—no time to reinvent the wheel. When they explained how to do something, I did it with all my energy and passion. This was a win-win situation for me.

Within a year I was number one in my distributorship and well on my way to being number one in the nation.

Tupperware would teach me how to sell a product that had a lifetime guarantee and that every household needed. All I had to do was find the people who would host a Tupperware party so I could sell it. It was that easy. I was bulletproof and everybody was my target.

After early successes, I came back to my distributor and asked what goals I should set for myself in order to be number one in the Austin area. How many parties would I need to book? How much Tupperware would I need to sell? How many new sales ladies do I need to recruit? What was it going to take for me to be number one? What kind of sales does it take to earn a car? The next stop— owning my first distributorship.

After I set my goals, I quickly learned how much of my time it really would take to be successful. I was working 16-hours a day and giving it 120 percent of my energy.

But, I was being rewarded for my efforts both financially and emotionally.

Within a year I was number one in my distributorship and well on my way to being number one in the nation.

Since there was really no down side to Tupperware, the only rejection I would get was from people who had other things going on in their lives. I was so determined to accomplish my goals I just would not let rejection slow me down. I just moved on and found the people who wanted Tupperware.

> *Rejection is a difficult thing to handle, especially when you're starting out in sales.*

Rejection is a difficult thing to handle, especially when you're starting out in sales. I was eight months pregnant and had gained a lot of weight. Typically, as sales parties would go, a woman would agree to host a party at her house and then she would invite a lot of her neighbors. Some of the time, the neighbors came only to help their friend or because they felt hooked in or pressured. Toward the end of this particular party it was my job to go around and get her friends to give additional parties. I was still young and inexperienced and very big and pregnant. I decided to approach three women sitting together. I knelt down and began asking them to book additional parties with me.

Rule number one – ladies find strength in numbers. Rule number two – pick out the weakest, most persuasive woman to ask first to get a "yes."

Well, I picked out the strongest, most negative neighbor and quickly got a firm "no." I then asked the other two women and all said "no." I needed more parties; I was tired, emotional and very upset. So I loaded all my unsold Tupperware into my station wagon and while I'm backing down the driveway I ran right over the hostess's mailbox, knocking the whole thing down. What else could go wrong? I was at that time #1 in the nation in Tupperware and couldn't book a party. I started to cry as I walked back into the house to tell the host of my accident. This is when my lucked changed. After telling everyone what I'd just done, all three of the women I had approached earlier felt so sorry for me they booked parties. This was success the hard way.

After you qualify and select your next team member you have to tell and show them you really care for them.

Team building was another lesson I had to learn and master to be successful in Tupperware.

After you qualify and select your next team member you have to tell and show them you really care for them. You have to also start teaching them the things they will need to be successful. I have found that shadowing is one of the best on-the-job training you can offer a new recruit. They have to observe you making a cold call on the phone, watch you introduce yourself to a stranger and make a sale or sign up a recruit. They need to be with you to watch and learn how to do all phases of the job. Hands-on instructing is much faster than classroom teaching.

The most important specialized sales skill I learned from Tupperware was public speaking. I had regular practice making speeches to just a few people to thousands.

Because of my success, energy and hard work, I got to speak at one of Tupperware's national conventions. That speech was the high point of my Tupperware career. I ended my speech with a story that truly showed how much the company had not only impacted my life but also my family's.

> *My daughter replied in her spookiest voice, "Tupperware."*

My parents had come over to see their grandchildren. I had to work late so my father offered to put my 4-year-old daughter to bed. My father was a great storyteller and my daughter asked for one that night. He started out with the common fairytale princess premise and then he made the story scary. He said, "We are walking down a winding path through the dark woods up to a rickety old house covered with moss. We knocked on the door and it slowly creaked open as we looked into the dark cottage. What do you think we saw?" My daughter replied in her spookiest voice, "Tupperware."

Lessons Learned

1. You must learn every aspect of your product in order to be successful at selling it.

2. You have to believe in your product to be successful.

3. You have to learn how to handle rejection.

4. You have to learn how to recruit and educate your team members.

5. You must learn how to become an effective public speaker. Practice, practice practice!

DING – DINNER IS SERVED!

My direct sales business had me pulling in long hours with most of that time spent on the phone, which forced me to schedule my presentations in the evenings. I was also a homemaker and the mother of a four-year-old son, Aaron and a seven-year-old daughter, Laura. I always had a laundry list of things to do and I never seemed to be able to make a dent in it. More often than not, I'd forget something. At the time, I bought into the 'pouch food' concept. For those of you who are not familiar with pouch food, let's just call it "a meal in a bag." All you had to do was pop it into the microwave and wait for the ding announcing that the food was ready. Once it was out of the microwave the kids could open their own pouch, with their own colored scissors, and squeeze. I used the microwave so much that every time the doorbell rang the kids would run looking for their scissors.

I remember one night in particular, when my son, Aaron was invited to his friend's house for dinner in our cul-de-sac. I was all for it—no pouches tonight! I was free to work on the phone, calling each member of my team.

After a few hours had passed, I heard the front door slam! He was back home.

The timing couldn't have been better. I had finished making my calls to my sales team. Aaron came running through the door with energy and excitement! He could barely speak. He rushed over to me and said he wanted to tell me something very important. As he looked up at me, he said "Mom, I just had the greatest thing ever!" I said "Great, well what was it?" You see, at this point in my life time was very valuable. Any tips or ideas on feeding the kids with good, fast, and of course, nutritious food was welcome.

He loved this special food so much, he wanted to make absolutely sure he got it right. He asked the neighbor to keep repeating it exactly, so he could repeat back to me exactly what it was. He kept asking her "What was it again?" Then he said, "Can you say this word very slowly so I can tell my mom?"

He had my attention. Now I was really curious; could it be something fancy, like beef stroganoff? Then Aaron looked up at me and said very slowly "...Mash-Po-Ta-Toes!"

Lesson Learned

Selling is sharing your stories, as I used this in my presentations. When we are being *transparent*, others can identify with us, connect with us, in juggling our family and career.

Chapter Three

Starting Over...How to Break Back Into Sales

One thing you will learn in life, if you haven't already, is success is not always a steady road upward.

After balancing a selling career with being a mother, I decided to quit my professional career and become a full-time mom. My children grew to become teenagers and then came an ugly divorce.

This was a very sad and painful time in my life. My children did not want for food, clothes or a roof over their heads; however, did they suffer. They suffered emotionally due to the anger and breakup of a family; that is, with a divorce. With the hurt and hardship on my kids and the pain we were all in, all I could do was pray that time could heal those wounds. And they were deep. This was the saddest time in my life.

> *One thing you will learn in life, if you haven't already, is success is not always a steady road upward.*

So here I was back in the business world having to support myself in a Ford Astro van, with no tape deck to listen to any motivational speakers and no power windows, a basic van to drive carpool. And I had to find a job. I could relate to SNL's Chris Farley's skit, the motivational speaker, living in a van down by the river. I was close.

Where there is a will there is a way, when your back is up against the wall.

I knew I could sell but had been out of the working world for 15 years. How could I get back into sales and what could I sell? Right off the bat, I was offered a sales position from a person I barely knew who owned retail clothing stores for women, in an upscale ladies boutique. I knew I would never have a day off, weekend or holiday (except Easter and Christmas of course) but with the competition for that type of business, it was always easy to be replaced by someone younger or anyone that needed it more than you did.

Now I loved clothes and like most women I was an expert at buying them. I just didn't know how to sell them! Where there is a will there is a way, when your back is up against the wall. Then I designed my own sales technique and it worked big time.

When I saw a customer looking for an outfit, I would quickly go to the back and put on the exact same outfit. The size of the customer did not matter as I dressed just like them in the same outfit.

I would then come running out to her and say, "Hey I think you would look great in this!" She would look at me and agree, the outfit really looked cute on me, and it must look cute on her too. And then it happened, she would go to the dressing room and I would pull her an outfit and me too. We both would get in the room and put our clothes on laughing, and look at each other and yell, "I love it!!" Literally get in the dressing room with her.

When we weren't the same size I knew how to use a belt and hang it lower or if they were smaller, make it fit tighter. I gave them what they wanted and began to teach them how to use and wear it well.

I was selling clothes and having fun.

After a few weeks I had my script and techniques down. But really I was still selling myself to people. Soon this became just another job to me. I knew I could not advance, own a store, have a franchise, as I had no money.

Thinking I really needed to find a product or service that I could be passionate about and be able to exert my energies into something people would want to really buy, I began to listen to people everywhere I went, and could be passionate about it.

I was working myself into the ground and driving this Astro van with no way to get a positive outlook on my situation by listening to those motivational tapes from years past.

Then I got a little help from a friend. My best girlfriend's husband called me up one day and told me he was going to sell his Lexus to me, for a deal. He said "There is no way you are going to be successful driving around in that VAN." He had been in sales his whole life and was very successful. He was right; I needed to up my game and image. You know the saying, "fake it until you make it."

I followed his advice. I was able to get a loan off my insurance company and a payment I could afford. Thank you State Farm!

Boy, did I start feeling successful riding around in this black sedan Lexus with tan interior. I decided no woman looks successful without having her nails done too.

So my next stop was a high-end nail salon. As I was sitting there getting my nails done, I overheard a nail technician tell a woman how she had lost weight and felt so much better since she started these nutritional products. I quickly leaned over and asked her what the name of the company was, and she told me—Body Wise International out of California.

> *That's right, I told them, "I am going to be your company's top salesperson in the country" and hung up.*

I couldn't wait to get home to my phone the next day to contact them, and did I ever! Once they answered I asked them "who do you have selling these products and are they in the fast lane?" "Nope, we do not have a race going on in that huge city of Houston." And that's when I told them my name and to write it down. That's right, I told them, "I am going to be your company's top salesperson in the country" and hung up. I was so excited when I hung up, I forgot to ask them how to get registered and get my products. I had a credit card and maxed it out for my DREAM of a lifetime.

The first thing I decided to do after I joined the company was to get a list of all of the most successful producers in their company. I then wanted to find out how they became successful and if they would consider mentoring me? I asked for their sales scripts and techniques and what they thought and believed made them successful. This was before cell phones, and believe me, I was really going to run up an expensive long distance phone bill. I had not even made one sale yet. Worse than that, I had a large credit card charge for the "Get Started Kits" I ordered, like $3000.00, that I would have to sell.

When all of this was happening, I had just remarried about a month before my whopping $400 phone bill came in the mailbox. I really didn't know how I was going to break this to my new husband as I slowly walked back to our apartment. He came home for lunch that day and I usually made him a sandwich, but not today.

The first thing I decided to do after I joined the company was to get a list of all of the most successful producers in their company.

When he sat down to eat it, I gently leaned over and said, "Hey honey, instead of having a sandwich how about let's go take a little "nap"? He jumped up out of his chair and with of course excitement, said, "A nap sounds great!" I made sure he got a really good nap, ha, and then showed him my phone bill. He looked at me for a minute and then he said, "Oh baby, everybody has start-up costs!"

It turned out that this direct nutrition sales company was a great fit for me. I believed in the products; they worked. I could be energetic and passionate about them. It was tailor-made for a hard driving salesperson like myself. I was off and running. I hit my sales goals and built my sales team by sharing my motivation and scripts. Their commission program was results driven. It rewarded us with bonuses, vacations and cars. I was driving an SL500 Mercedes, and knew my children would see all of my hard efforts to be successful for them.

When you believe in your company and its products, there is no limit to your success.

It was so great to drive up to my retail stores, and see my friend, Karen McCullough, the owner, and who I had worked for in those cute boutiques. She couldn't believe my success in such a short time. She yelled at me, "You know nothing about nutrition and weight loss!" And then it happened...she wanted to sign up with me! I told her to sell enough to go to San Diego and Leadership school...and she did.

And that's when she kicked off her speaking career, on the bus entertaining everyone. See, I told her that's what I did, on the BUS. Made everyone laugh at themselves, that their credit cards were UNBELIEVABLE! Use words to describe my life, one word...and it worked.

What she didn't know is that I had become a student of my products. So much so that I was responsible for opening up an entire new market sector for the company, launching Texas into the medical field of nutritional products. When you believe in your company and its products, there is no limit to your success. I was bulletproof and I could sell to anyone. I loved people, mentoring others, wanting them to have success... teaching them that their talents were unlimited.

Funny story, and an example of your own sales ability—it is right there in front of you. We were headed to California on a business trip, and in a store at the airport. Just glancing around, a magazine cover caught my eye. It was clear as a bell what it said on the cover—"How to fly first class without paying for it." Wow, I was in. I grabbed that magazine, turned to the article, and paid up. Told my husband, let's go to the gate and upgrade, I have the steps. You see, I just read the four steps to follow on "how to fly first class without paying for it."

He told me to calm down and that we would need points to make this happen. I just said to follow me, do exactly what I said the steps said, as I had just read the article on the how-to.

We approached the departure gates desk and I began telling the attendant exactly what the article suggested me to say. I first told her

> *You should be wanting to give people a positive and pleasant reason to want to keep you in their lives.*

that we only fly this airline, and I was watching her to see if she could check to see if we had enough airmiles to be bumped up to first class.

I already knew we didn't. The attendant looked us up on the screen and said, "Oh Mrs. Hopper, you are a bronze member and you don't have enough points to fly first class." Then she continued, "It's going to cost you and your husband $150.00 each to bump up to the next level." The article said my reply should be, "Oh, I am so disappointed." "We only fly this airline, and we're really trying to build our air miles up but it seems it's going to take FOREVER."

I thanked her and did exactly what the next step was, to be very disappointed walking away. As we sat down my husband looked at me and said, "Well, how'd that work out for you?" I whispered back, saying "We have NOT finished the article steps yet! Keep your head down and look very sad." My husband said, "Okay, but I told you so." And then it happened, here she came, walking over to us with two first class tickets. Music to my ears—"Mr. and Mrs. Hopper, we would love to offer you both first class tickets without using any of your airmiles or money."

1. When you have an opportunity, don't hesitate and move quickly to make your presentation.

2. Don't over think things!

3. Go by scripts.

4. Scripts are for professionals.

You should be wanting to give people a positive and pleasant reason to want to keep you in their lives.

Working on friendships and making time for people will always pay you great dividends.

Lastly, be prepared to ask, as ASKING IS NOT SELLING, and you will open your world up ten-fold!

BOB, CAROL, TED AND ALICE CAME TO VISIT IN THE NIGHT

I had just started my newest endeavor, selling vitamins and minerals, also called AMs and PMs because you take your minerals at night and the vitamins in the morning. One particular evening during my presentation, I noticed a strange-acting man in the back of the room pacing back and forth and smoking. He never sat down and never looked directly at me but would just quickly glance in my direction. At one point he tried to light a cigarette and then turned and hurried out of the room.

It didn't help that I was there by myself and had a long drive home and was thinking he was going to kill me. By the end of my presentation I had become so unnerved that I told a friend to throw a party at my funeral. The good news was, I sold a ton of product.

At the end of the evening I packed up my remaining products and presentation equipment and headed to my car. I was so freaked out by this guy that I had a friend come with me while I loaded everything in my trunk. I even looked under my car just to be safe. I couldn't stop looking in my rearview mirror all the way home to see if he was following me.

Thank goodness I made it home safe and sound. The following morning I received a phone call from a woman who was very upset. She had attended my presentation the night before and purchased a set of AM/PM vitamins for her son. She said I might remember him because he was the man standing and pacing in the back of the room. I thought: Oh, yeah, him, the one that was going to kill me? She explained that her son had schizophrenia and she thought the vitamins and minerals might help him. She had given him the PM minerals that night before he went to bed. The next morning, he said that four people came into bed with him. (This is weird but true...you can't make this stuff up.) She went on saying that he never had anything like that happen before and she wanted her money back. I said once the bottle had been opened we can't take them back. She told me I didn't understand. After he took the PM vitamins and went to bed and four people showed up! Could it be Bob, Carol, Ted and Alice? She said this was the first time four people showed up! Like I said, you can't make this stuff up!

I got very nervous. I thought I was the cause of this. I sold the vitamins to her and worried that she just might try and sue me and my company. Maybe they would fire me. I told her to hold on. I scrambled looking for her check. I asked her to flush the minerals down the commode and to listen as I tore up her check. After hanging up with her I quickly called my husband and told him what happened. I wondered if I had done the right thing. He paused for a minute and said, "It sounds like you didn't sell them enough... you should have sold her four more sets for Bob, Carol, Ted and Alice."

Lesson Learned

Always qualify your client to purchase.

Chapter Four

Building Good Business Relationships

I think the best way to be successful is to continually search for and build good business relationships. These relationships develop into gifts that keep on giving. A good business relationship will help you be successful in your present job and often helps to build your career in the future.

> *The best way to be successful is to continually search for and build good business relationships.*

This is what exactly happened to me. I was busy building my direct sales career in Houston when I got a phone call from a group of investors that were putting together a startup company in Las Vegas. The company would be a direct sales company that would manufacture and sell their unique line of women's nutritional supplements and skin care products. They made me an offer to be the chief executive officer of their new company. This offer would be a great career move for me but also have a big impact on my family and lifelong friendships. My husband and I discussed it. I prayed about it. I asked advice from my family and friends. It turned out it was a good time for us to make such a move in our lives.

Besides being very positive for my career, my husband accepted a job as a project executive with the Venetian Hotel and Casino. All of our kids had graduated, had jobs and were living on their own. With a little more thought we concluded the timing for the move was perfect. In fact, we should move as quickly as possible before any of the kids started thinking about moving back in.

In this chapter I would like to use this business startup story to give you some real techniques and strategies on how to be successful in sales.

What could be better for my sales career than having the "Nancy Hopper Show" coming to you live from Las Vegas, Nevada?

The first few question of new company's marketing plan were easy to answer.

Define your products as well as your target markets. Our products were nutritional supplements and women's skin care creams. Our target market was a woman—all women.

The question of how we were going to market our products took a little more research and time. Our marketing plan to the public was a combination of a sales force using direct network marketing backed up with radio and print advertising.

Print advertising was pretty standard. We brought in an ad agency that created some catchy and colorful advertising. They then purchased space in the local newspapers and magazines.

Our radio ads were a bit more involved and exciting. I chose to create and produce a weekly hour-long call-in show for women's health and beauty tips. This was a very exciting, motivating learning experience for me. What could be better for my sales career than having the "Nancy Hopper Show" coming to you live from Las Vegas, Nevada? That was truly a blast and one of the highlights of my Las Vegas experience.

The first thing a customer buys is you!

One of the most important parts of a direct sales marketing company is their compensation plan. The accountants and the startup company's investors handled that part of the business/marketing plan.

The next most important part of a direct sale and marketing company was to develop a strong and productive sales force.

Here is where one of my fundamental business strategies paid off. "The best way to be successful in sales is to build good business relationships."

I had to build numerous strong business relationships in the direct sales and network market industry. Because of this, I was able to put together a strong and productive sales group. Having these relationships, I knew who would be a good fit for my company and product. Then all I had to do was call and find out if the timing was right for them. My sales team came together very quickly.

Next came the harder part of marketing my new company and its products. I had to go after what I call the "cold market." My definition of the cold market is selling to someone you don't know or selling to someone that does not know about your product.

This is where a sales person shows his ability to sell. How do you do this?

You can be as successful in sales as you want to be.

The first and most important part of selling is that you have to know your product, what your customer is buying. This is usually a salesman's first mistake. *The first thing a customer buys is you!* You are the one unique thing in the selling process. Therefore, you have to make sure you and everything about yourself is ready for the sale. PUT YOUR GAME FACE ON.

How do you get yourself ready to sell yourself first?

Let's start with the easiest part of you. Prepare to be sold.

The Physical You

When God made you, you arrived here on earth with some basic characteristics that you can't do much about. Your height, the size of your head, the length of your arms, the length of your legs, the size of your feet and hands are for the most part not changeable. Pretty much everything else we can work or have worked on to change to our liking or acceptance.

Whether we like it or not our basic animalistic instincts and our social norms determine what we find attractive. We can choose to work toward these standards of acceptance or choose to try and redefine these standards.

You need to get back to the basics of acceptance and being attractive to your potential new customer. You can surely be clean, well groomed and well dressed.

I have this little verse sitting on my mirror stand in the bathroom that says "I will look as good as I possibly can to anyone that sees me today."

Fact: Size does matter. The more overweight you are the more unhealthy you will become. Being overweight is a negative drawback in sales. But the good news is that there's a way you can compensate for most physical, social and/or intellectual disadvantages. You can be as successful in sales as you want to be. I will share this career-changing secret a little later in this book.

Unless you are an old pro, you need to have a plan.

Sadly to say, most, if not all, marketing, social and professional networking events are the unhealthiest places you could ever go to eat or drink. Here is a little advice. Try not to eat or drink at these networking functions. Give your pancreas and liver a break. It is a way to stand out, be different from the herd. Standing out is attractive to most people; they see it as strength. If you do have to have something in your hand get yourself a tonic water or soda with a lime so they think you are drinking a vodka! The next meeting someone will be copying you!

Like I said, the physical preparation for a network event is the easy part. How you prepare yourself mentally and emotionally is a little harder. Unless you are an old pro, you need to have a plan. There are rules for success and tripping points that will cause you to fail.

In Las Vegas when every event was a cold situation, I went back and tried proven successful networking techniques. I have used these techniques over and over in every type of networking group situations.

First let's go over a few DON'TS. You don't go to a networking event to:

1. See how many people you can speak to.

2. To talk to everybody you already know.

3. To be the life of the party.

4. To tell jokes and entertain people.

5. To have a couple of drinks, relax and be seen

6. To see how many business cards you can give out

I find a way to say my name at least three times to each person I meet.

Remember, your purpose is to meet someone new, see if they qualify as a potential customer or client, and most importantly, leave the encounter with the person you have just met wanting to know more about you and wanting to see you again. This is no small accomplishment for a few minutes of conversation.

So here you have just valeted your car and are walking up to the sign-in table. The first thing you do is to print your name as large and as bold as you can on the nametag. You then stick the nametag on your right lapel, NOT YOUR LEFT LAPEL. That's where everyone else usually sticks his or hers. Why the right lapel? When you introduce yourself and shake a person's hand, you use your right hand, which causes them to have to look at the right side of your body. Also, wearing the nametag on the right might catch someone's eye because most people wear their nametags on their left.

So now you have your nametag on and your business cards in your pocket and you are ready to work the room. It suddenly comes to you that you don't know a single soul and you are here all by yourself.

I listen and observe who is speaking, who has energy, and who has chemistry with me.

It's natural to come into a room of strangers and be nervous. First thing you have to tell yourself is we are all here for the same purpose. Everyone is here to meet other people, so introducing yourself is really the normal and expected thing to do. So what do you do? You have to start by getting your name out there. You don't sit down and you don't go stand by another lonely person who has been cut out from the herd. Without hesitation you go right up to the largest group and introduce yourself. People first have to know and remember your name. Therefore, I find a way to say my name at least three times to each person I meet. Here is an example of how such a conversation would go.

I look over the group standing there. I am looking for a person or persons that I would want to build a relationship with. I am looking for potential clients who are going to be perfect and fun people. So I listen and observe who is speaking, who has energy, and who has chemistry with me. I pick a person and say, "Hi, my name is Nancy Hopper." She introduces herself and the others in her group. As I'm told each person's name, I look them in the eye and give each one a firm handshake and repeat their name as well as my own name. Now I have a different problem, I have just talked to four people and can only remember two of their names. Good thing everyone is wearing a nametag. So I then pick out two of them, go back to them and ask what company they are with or what they do. If I think there might be a fit I tell them what I do and hand them my business card.

You show you care by asking questions and being attentive to find out what their wants and needs are.

Again, I tell them I want you to remember my name. I say their name again—so your name is Julie right? (I repeat) that I am Nancy Hopper. I then will use word association. My name is Hopper like the actor Dennis Hopper. Or I might say Hopper like the Energizer bunny hop-hop-hopping along. I hop everywhere! I say whatever I think will get their attention. Then if I really like Julie I would laughingly turn to her and say I want you to remember my name so say it three times, quickly. Everyone laughs and I move on to the next group.

So I now have talked to a couple of people during the night and have picked out three to four people I would like to follow up with. So before I leave I will go back to each of them. I will first pick out something about how they look. I'll notice if they are blonde or brunette, tall or short, funny or serious. Things like this help me remember them later. I would look at their business card again. So on my way out I would go by them again, say their name, repeat my name, give them a compliment or say something funny. She would laugh and I would say it was great to meet you and I am going to call you. So don't forget my name – Nancy Hopper. By the time the night is over I have already started to form a good connection with a few of the women and from their response, the feeling is mutual. A successful night of networking will produce the basis for a couple of new relationships.

In the days following the networking function, I follow up and make an appointment to talk with them again. You mustn't wait too long to do this or your efforts at the function will have been in vain. As you can see or already know, effective and productive networking is hard work. You have to be attentive and energetic during the introduction phase.

This is the Secret – "Humor and Laughter."

When you are following up with them you now have to really start selling yourself. You have to show them you actually care for them. If not, it shows. People can tell if you are insincere.

You show you care by asking questions and being attentive to find out what their wants and needs are. To do this you have to like the people you are networking with. This may sound funny, but you have to learn to care for potential clients. You have to find out what they need and exactly what they're looking for. Next, you want to try and see if you can help them fulfill those wants and needs. After you have accomplished this and they have "bought you," you need to figure out if your product matches their needs.

After the sale, you need to keep them in your center of influence and keep them buying from you and recommending to do the same. To do this you need to show them that they will lose something good in their life if you are not a part of it. This something is emotional and it's a feeling. It's intangible.

What is this feeling that can keep a business relationship going? You have to bring some sort of joy or pleasant feeling to them. A good salesperson is a person who projects a pleasant, energetic and caring personality with "Humor and Laughter." This type of person can bring a feeling of joy to a professional relationship. THIS IS THE SECRET – "HUMOR AND LAUGHTER." Joy can compensate for almost any type of disadvantage two people can have between them. Whether it is social, physical, demographic or intellectual, humor can bridge the difference and bring joy to the relationship.

Have you ever wondered why sales are so hard and why there are so few good successful salespeople? The sad fact is there are not that many people out in the business world that really care about others. They don't want to bring happiness to their clients' lives or careers. Give people joy in their lives and they will buy you and anything you are selling.

Lessons Learned

1. Fall in love with people.

2. Say your name at least three times to people you are meeting for the first time.

3. Include humor and laughter in your sales relationships.

4. Follow up quickly with people you meet and show them you care.

JOHNNY BENCH TO THE MAX!

As my Mother and I were boarding a plane to Phoenix, AZ to hop over to Durango, CO to see my son. As I we were sitting on the plane in coach, two very excited little boys were talking about seeing Johnny Bench in first class. I had no idea who Johnny Bench was so I didn't give it much thought until one of the boys was seated next to me. He was telling his mother that Johnny Bench was ten rows ahead of us. Now, I had to ask him "Who is Johnny Bench?"

The boy looked surprised that I didn't know he was a famous baseball catcher who played for the Cincinnati Reds and that he was a fourteen time all-star and in the National Baseball Hall of Fame. But what really seemed to excite him was the next bit of information. He raised his little hand and said "he's the only man on earth that can hold seven baseballs in one hand!"

Once we got airborne, I grabbed a pen and two business cards—one to give to him and one to get an autograph for my son, Aaron Ace who loved baseball. I told my mother to move her little bitty legs and let me out of our row. She said, "Oh no, Nancy, don't go!" I then walked up the aisle and headed straight to where the only guy in first class had a baseball cap on. It had to be Johnny Bench.

Once I got there, I knelt down, looking at him in his face. I asked him, "Are you the famous Johnny Bench who can hold seven baseballs in one hand?" And he smiled and said, "Yes." Then I immediately noticed an elderly lady next to him and asked quietly, "is that your wife?" With a big smile on my face. He looked at me with a frown on his face and said "...NOOOOOO!" We laughed and then he said, "Are you married?" "Seriously, you know I'm married," and we began to laugh! My next big question was, "What are you doing with your life after baseball now?" He told me he was speaking, signing autographs and looking for products he could endorse. I can't believe it! I said, "I am with a nutritional company in California and they just happen to be looking for a celebrity spokesperson." I told him that if he purchased my products, he could have his own residual income. I was on fire now. I knew my time was limited since I was blocking the aisle so I quickly asked him for his number to contact him. And of course would he please sign my business card to my son with his autograph. Then Johnny (we were on first name basis by this time) gave me a number to contact his manager. As I went to take his card and number, he quickly pulled it back. He said he would give me the card under one condition: that I would not tell the little boys in the back of the plane who he was. I agreed and told him I was looking forward to talking to his manager next week.

As I got up to walk back, I had to open the drape that separated coach from first class. And there they were, those little boys' faces looking right at me, and I mouthed the words, silently: "That's Johnny Bench!" I could not hold back my own excitement, and they came running to get his autograph.

As my Mom and I were walking through the airport headed to baggage claim, I saw him meet his driver on the other side of the jetway. I yelled out at him, jumping up and down, and said, "Johnny, it's me, Nancy Hopper and this is my mother, Mary!"

He put his large hands to his mouth, and yelled back to us, "MARY, MY CONDOLENCES!"

Later that next week I called his manager and as what can happen in business, things did not work out with him and my company. But that story I used in all of my sales career to help others build confidence in stepping out of their comfort zone and going for the introduction.

1. Do not hesitate to introduce yourself or product to a potential client (famous or not).

2. Asking is NOT SELLING.

3. You will have a story to share every time.

BREAKING BAD – GET OUT OF YOUR COMFORT ZONE!

I had just been to a truly motivating sales conference in California and was flying home all pumped up with awards and new products to sell. I found my seat and was struggling to get my carry-on into the overhead storage compartment. Right when I was about to give up, a handsome man in his 40s came to my rescue. I thanked him and we both found our seats. Little did he know my salesperson radar had just identified him. He didn't know it, but he had entered the three-foot rule; Step 1, he looked me in the eyes. Step 2, he came within 3 feet of me. And Step 3, he engaged me in a polite conversation.

Once the sign "You are free to move about the cabin" came on, the man sitting next to him got up and went to the bathroom. That was my chance. I quickly walked back to his seat and sat down by my new friend. I quickly introduced myself as did he. After just a few minutes of pleasantries, I learned about Steve's family. He had three kids; the youngest being a six-month-old little girl. I told him about my older kids and what a satisfying feeling it was to see them grow up and start developing into young adults. I then asked if he was looking forward to that and he said yes. We talked about the importance of staying healthy and exercising. Steve then shared with me his own health concerns. He was struggling with high cholesterol and was taking a drug to keep it in a safe range. I was then able to introduce him to a new and all natural product my company had just developed that lowered cholesterol levels. He was very excited to try it. But at that moment the other man had returned and wanted his seat back. I quickly introduced myself to him and went back to my seat. Boy, was I passionate about my company's new nutritional product, and it showed. I was in the zone. I was pumped about my company, my products and my ability to sell.

I told my new friend, Steve, that once we got off the plane I would need to get his name, address and credit card information. I would then have the product shipped to him within days.

While we were standing on the jetway exchanging information, I realized that my passion and excitement for my company's new products was contagious. Jeff, the man seated next to Steve, stopped and gave me his name and credit card information so I could mail him the same product. I was on a roll, but it only got better. A woman seated behind Steve and Jeff came up to me and handed me a note with her name and credit card number. She said she couldn't help but overhear our conversation and wasn't completely sure what I was selling but wanted in on the action.

To even make things better, my husband was waiting for me and saw all three people come up to me for the sale. He knew I was a good salesperson but seeing three people stop me on the jetway for my product gave me even more validation.

Lesson Learned

Get out of your comfort zone and engage! You never know who you are going to meet, even on a plane!

LAUNCHING MY NEW SKIN CARE COMPANY

This is a quick story about how if you earn people's trust by helping them obtain the goals and filling their needs, it becomes a win-win situation for everybody.

I had built up a sizable sales team and group of product customers in Houston, Texas. To celebrate, I put on a girls night out fashion shop, provided product booths for other companies' products and had great music and finger food for all. It was a great night at the Houston Junior League ballroom. After a time for shopping at the booths, the fashion show and time to let everyone network I made a big announcement. I told everyone that I was starting a new company told everyone in the room that if they were interested in being a part of this endeavor they needed to fill out the new company membership forms at their tables and give me their credit card information. Everyone was excited and pumped more than usual. Many were coming up to me, congratulating me on the new company and thrilled that they could be a part of it. No questions asked! Except for one woman sitting in the very back of the room. She raised her hand and said in an apologetic voice, "Nancy, excuse me, what is it exactly that we are selling?" She said she didn't know any of the details but that she filled out the forms and gave me her credit card information

Lesson Learned

Enthusiasm is contagious!

THE MAGIC BULLET

Today one of my companies is a nutritional wellness clinic where I coach people in their journey to weight loss. One of the most challenging things a person can do is change the way they deal with food. Many of my clients need more than just a diet plan, they need a lifestyle change which is a perfect match with my coaching skills.

I walk every new client through my program which entails introducing them to all of the food options and how to prepare them. I have puddings, shakes, soups, omelets, desserts, etc. that are all made from a protein powder and must be mixed with an exact amount of water to come out in the right texture and form. I give each client a shaker which I simply call "the magic bullet" because it helps make the preparation easy. I also give them a list of dos and don'ts, and before they leave I make sure to schedule an appointment for the following week to track their progress and answer any questions they might have.

I had a very attractive woman in her forties start the program. I was meeting with her after her first week on the diet. I was so excited to see how she did and how she liked the foods. When I asked how often she used the Magic Bullet and did it make things easier for her she gave me a strange look and told me she used it twice that week. I said "Twice in one week? You should be using it twice a day!" I told her this this is a lifestyle change. She looked very embarrassed.

That's when it hit me. She wasn't referring to my Magic Bullet but to her "other magic bullet," the one that vibrates. We laughed so hard our faces hurt.

Lesson Learned

Communication is everything. The ability to laugh at yourself is priceless.

Chapter Five

Building On Your Success

Looking back at my years in Las Vegas, I worked hard to get my new company up and running. I had filled all of the required personnel and officers positions. I had installed all of the company's programs and procedures. We were able to make payroll, pay our taxes and best of all, our new products were selling.

Now that we had a little breathing room, we could focus on developing a loyal customer base that would purchase from us on a regular basis. This helped pay the bills while we were continuing to grow and find new customers. We were now building on our success while still living within our projected operating budgets.

Happy, contented customers are good promotional tools that will help build a larger base.

How does a company retain their customers while building an even larger base? To start with, you need to first go with the standard good business practices, techniques and strategies.

First, you need to make sure you really know your existing customers. To do this you will need to survey them to obtain updated market data concerning your products.

Next, you must change how you interface with your existing customers. When you were first introducing them to your products and company, you just focused on them and their needs. You would tell them just to concentrate on making the product work for them (the new customer). You really don't want them telling others about the products. You were totally focused on your customer.

Successful sales stories will increase your bottom line faster than any other sales strategies.

Now that these customers are a part of your loyal base, both of you can start enjoying additional benefits from this relationship. Creating a customer bonus and discount program can do this. You contact your existing customers and give them the details of the program. You explain how the company will give them a discount on their future purchase or an actual cash bonus for sending new customers their way. How great is that? It's a win-win situation for all.

Happy, contented customers are good promotional tools that will help build a larger base. Over the years I have found that successful sales stories will increase your bottom line faster than any other sales strategies. This goes back to the old salespersons' adage – "Facts tell. Stories sell." Nothing helps sales better than a good story of how a big and important customer bought your product and got great results.

The following is a perfect example:

My husband and I were in Baton Rouge visiting my in-laws. Mel, my husband, had to run a few errands so I stayed back to visit with my brother-in-law. You see, he and Mel played football for LSU and my brother-in-law loved to tell stories about his glory days. On this particular visit I had listened to one too many. I picked up a magazine sitting on the table and boy, what I read next got me excited. I jumped up and grabbed my brother-in-law's hand and said "Let's drive out to LSU and get the whole team on my nutritional products." I had just read that a Texas football team was put on an Amway product. I thought to myself, well I can do better than that. I could put the whole LSU football program on my products.

My brother-in-law thought I was crazy but took me out to the campus. LSU is a big college and has a very large campus. He could not believe I would actually try and sell my vitamins to the LSU football program. He thought it was such a large organization that it would be close to impossible to talk to a decision maker that day. As we were getting out of the car to head over to the football offices, guess who walked right passed us? The head football coach for LSU. When my brother-in-law pointed him out, I took off running. I scissor jumped across a hedge and came face to face with the coach. I stuck out my hand and gave him a good strong shake as I said, "Coach, my name is Nancy Hopper and you don't know me, but my husband and this guy right here played football for LSU a number of years ago." He said, "OK great." I

I jumped up and grabbed my brother-in-law's hand and said "Let's drive out to LSU and get the whole team on my nutritional products."

replied, "That's not why I'm here. I'm here to see if I could sit down with you for a few minutes and tell you about a nutritional product line I am with. One in particular promotes more oxygen to the blood cells. It's great for athletes and the pill isn't manufactured in a hot press. It is made using a cold process, which also helps it dissolve quickly and get into the blood stream faster." Then I said "I know you have a big game coming up with Alabama, right?" He took a minute and looked at me and tells me to follow him to his office. My brother-in-law's mouth is now wide open and he's in complete shock.

The great thing about positive experiences is that they seem to build on each other.

As we sit down I begin to show him the ingredients list on the bottle. Thank God I had that bottle on me. I began explaining how quickly this product dissolves and goes right into the blood stream. A football player could take it before a game and not feel so exhausted. It is not a drug and is an all-natural vitamin. He said "OK." I asked "How many players will you be giving this to?" and he told me, "enough bottles for the whole team!" I asked for his credit card and told him I'd have the bottles shipped to his office right away.

I showed him my product, asked for the sale and gave him a reason to purchase it. Then I promised the value in it. We laughed and I told him I would be coming back to the game and would be on the 45th yard line.

I was really pumped, not only for a huge sale, but for the credibility it gave my product line and me. Also, I loved it when he called me after the winning game against

Alabama. We had a good talk and he thanked me again. He said his players said they could really tell a difference.

I cannot calculate how much product this one story has sold for me. It gave me an immeasurable amount of credibility. This story produced more product sales than any other advertising or promotions project I was ever involved with. This was certainly was one of the highlights in my sales career. The great thing about positive experiences is that they seem to build on each other.

Right after my LSU football experience I jumped right back into staying out of my comfort zone again.

Lessons Learned

1. Confirmation of the classic salesman's advice – Facts Tell and Stories Sell.

2. Confirms that cold calling and getting out of your comfort zone works!

Chapter Six

Cold Calling

Have you ever had any success in "cold calling"?

For those who have heard of the process but aren't really clear on what it is, it is important to note that the person on the other end of the phone has no desire whatsoever to talk to you. They are not interested in your product, your service or whatever you are selling...and at this point they have no interest in you.

No matter the trade, service, product, or skill, you have been gifted and there are millions of people looking specifically for you.

And yet, this is how business is generated... this is how business moves. If there was a compass that was used for your business in getting it off the ground, it would not be about North, West, East or South...it would be about getting on a phone, making a call and hoping to goodness someone gives you more than the five seconds they desire to give for you to share what you have to offer.

Cold calling requires someone who is focused and determined. Believe me, these are not one and the same. You can start off with a focused mind that nothing is going to stop you in generating business, but your determination can die down quite quickly if you have the phone slammed in your ear time and time again.

This is what separates the girls from the women: staying with it, focused on it and not letting your emotions get in the way.

Cold calling requires someone who is focused and determined.

Now, let's be honest...times have changed; what used to be an office to office call has become a home to home call, a home to beach call, a home to car call and many other variations because the computer has changed business. It has given us an opportunity to work in our pajamas even though we may manage millions of dollars in purchasing power.

I want you to know and understand that success is possible. You can become just as I became...a successful person in business. No matter the trade, service, product, or skill, you have been gifted and there are millions of people looking specifically for you.

You must believe this or you might as well give up.

Don't do that! Ha!

Let's make some money! Let's have some fun and let's ride the journey through this book that I have shared my secrets in and you can learn how to achieve no matter the opposition.

I did.

In this book, I have summarized the lessons and techniques that I have learned over the years; I have taught you how to visualize your tasks that lay ahead and to visualize the success you will make after making your first contact, going through your first presentation and closing that deal and making it a great step in developing a long and successful business partnership!

This commitment only begins by practicing and growing as it won't "just happen"!

I am not trying to be a taskmaster. I just want you all to discover like I did that there is a whole new world out there for all of who have the gitty-up to make it happen, and this book is going to be the best purchase you will make or have made as it relates to earning the income and living the lifestyle you desire.

Heck, I remember standing in front of my bathroom mirror, over and over again, practicing my acceptance speech in my company for being top in sales, even though at that time I had not accomplished it.

Business is about action.

I had and I had to have just like you are going to have to have...the vision, the dream while seeing the success was right there in front of me; and you are going to have to do the same thing. All I had to do was to get moving.

Business is about action. Learning is an action, running a company, is an action, and all of us can become leaders. So don't over think things...open up your heart and mind to something new, something wonderful and something inviting. But also know that we may trip, stumble and fall in the process; this is where the determining factor will either stay with you or you will give up...

There's a statement, "It's not the words we say, it's the music we play." Allow your stumbles be a new dance for you, partner with these mistakes and allow them to stay with you so you can see how far you have come and to use them to help others, because giving back is what it is all about...earn and learn...and give, right?

This was the beginning for me. That practice went into cold calling, making appointments, presenting presentations, meeting one on one with a prospect and closing them!

I shared with you the "one secret" which again is having humor, laughter and building these strong relationships with your clients, who will become your friends! I am totally honored and grateful that my friends and audiences throughout my professional career still RELATE, REMEMBER AND RETELL my stories! Now I have put all of this information in my book.

This book gives you a written path to success. I hope this path will make your success a little easier by learning what works without having to experience what doesn't work.

Good Luck!

Share your stories with me soon! We are all on this journey together!

The REAL SECRET is to be a little bit CRAZY, Be DRIVEN by PURPOSE and bring an ATTITUDE SECOND TO NONE!

My Mother

Who fed me from her gentle breast,
And hush'd me in her arms to rest,
And on my cheek sweet kisses pressed,
My Mother

When sleep forsook my open eye,
Who was it sung sweet hushaby,
And rock'd me that I should not cry?
My Mother

Who sat and watched my infant head,
When sleeping in my cradle bed,
And tears of sweet affection shed?
My Mother

When pain and sickness made me cry,
Who gazed upon my heavy eye,
And wept for fear that I should die?
My Mother

Who dress'd my doll in clothes so gay,
And taught me pretty how to play.
And minded all I had to say?
My Mother

Who taught my infant lips to pray,
And love God's holy book each day.
And walk in Wisdom's pleasant way?
My Mother

Who's Behind the Curtain for You?

And can I ever cease to be
Affectionate and kind to thee,
Who was so very kind to me?
My Mother

Ah, no! The thought I cannot bear,
And if God please my life to spare,
I hope I shall reward thy care,
My Mother

Who ran to help me when I fell,
And would some pretty story tell,
Or kiss the place to make it well?
My Mother

When thou art feeble, old and gray,
My healthy arm shall thy stay,
And I will soothe thy pains away,
My Mother

And when I see thee hang thy head,
'Twill be my turn to watch thy head
And tears of sweet affection shed,
My Mother

For could our Father in the skies
Look down with pleasure or loving eyes,
If ever I could dare despise
My Mother

Ann Taylor (1783-1866)
Poet and literary critic

Made in the USA
Columbia, SC
18 September 2018